ME AND MY ECONOMY

Published by
Lotus Press

ME AND MY ECONOMY

VEENA VERMA

M.A. (Economics), M.Ed.

Former -Principal

(Directorate of Education, Delhi Administration, Delhi)

Lotus PRESS

4263/3, Ansari Road,

Darya Ganj, New Delhi-110 002

Lotus Press
4263/3, Ansari Road, Darya Ganj,
New Delhi-110002 • Ph.: 32903912, 23280047
E-mail: lotus_press@sify.com • www.lotuspress.co.in

ME AND MY ECONOMY

ISBN: 978-81-8382-242-8

Published by: Lotus Press, New Delhi

Printed at: Anand Sons, Delhi

Acknowledgements

I would like to express my sincere thanks
for the Blessings of
My Spiritual Guru
Sant Jaganath Gothi
and My Gurumantra
Om Sachchidanand Nahma
and
My GuruMaa

Preface

The book *Me and My Economy* aims at the knowledge of the word Economy to a layman. Whether you are a student of economics or not, whether you have ever studied economics or not, either you are a farmer or an agriculturist, either you are an entrepreneur or an industrialist, either you are a rickshaw-puller or a travelers company, either you are a shop keeper or a big businessman, either you are a banker or a financial company, either you are a politician or a voter, either you are an engineer or a labourer, either you are a soldier or a commander. In other words, from a layman class to a higher job class, and further, a glamorous class, it is essential for all of us to know the meaning of the word economy and economics.

It is because each and every individual matters to an economy. They contribute to their economy and they are an integral part of their economy. So what I am to my economy and what an economy is to me? How much I am important for my economy and how much my economy is important for me? These concepts must be understood deeply by each and every individual of an economy. Then only the layman class will elect the worthy and responsible leaders to whom they hand over their economy.

The author's aim of this book is to realize the importance of the subject Economics at 10+2 level as an independent stream and not only as a sub-discipline of social science. The subject Economics is not being given importance to that extent as it should have been given. As the students of the fifth standard know about the subjects Hindi, English, Maths, Science, Social Studies, and Drawing, he does not know what Economics is? Social Science may include History and Geography, but Economics should be treated as an independent separate subject.

Presently Economics is not treated as an independent stream. It is a sub-discipline of Social-Science at 10+2 level, and at the university level it is treated as a subject under Commerce and Management Courses. And very few courses are there under Economics. This is the reason why we name large numbers of M.B.A. colleges. These MBA colleges are producing commercial and professional brains whereas a college of Economics will produce not only commercial and professional brains, but also economically sound all round developed brains.

Today all our youths are running after Business Administrations; no problem, but preparing our youths for Economics Administration is more important. In whole India there is only one school of economics and that is Delhi School of Economics. It is not sufficient. The subject which should get utmost importance, is getting very little importance. So there is need to open schools and colleges of Economics not only in India but in the whole world.

The study of Economics Administration must be made compulsory for all leaders, netas, politicians and ministers. They should be given proper training to manage their economy.

The uneducated leaders taking oath and becoming minister are just playing with the Economy and not handling properly an economy. Hence they should undergo a proper training program under Economics Administration and Economy Management.

Lastly, the aim of this book is to give a message to the masses of the world that they should learn to nourish their economy by contributing their services not only for professional and personal motives, but also for improving and progressing their economy as a whole also.

We should not learn to exploit our resources for our selfish motives, but we should learn to nourish our Economy in all respects for the whole economy, for each and every sector and for each and every individual.

"I wish if the services of Education shoudn't have been commercialised."

—Veena Verma

Content

Content

1

"A Layman's Economics"

Does Economics, such an important and useful subject, exists only for economists, educationists. Policy-makers, statisticians, and planning commission only? Does an economy stands on the shoulders of these few categories? No, absolutely not. Every Economy is standing on the shoulders of its layman class. Then how come a layman doesn't know its meaning and importance?

Thus it is very important for a layman to know the meaning and importance of Economics. He should know his contribution towards his economy.

For a layman:

An Economy is a system which provides you money for the work you have done, you have contributed either in the form of goods or services. You are a very important factor of production for your economy. Every layman who is a part of the working force of its economy, contributes to its economy and gets back its return in the form of the factor of income.

The layman's proportion in the total population is highest, say about 70-75 percent, but this layman class does not even know its role, its responsibility, its contribution, its importance '"nothing. They come to know their importance at the time of elections only. And when the elections are over, their role in the economy is also over. Therefore, they need to know the importance of their role in the economic growth of their economy. If the laymen class is trained in such a manner and if this behavior is cultivated in them, that their Economy depends on their economic behavior mainly, then they can definitely be moulded and prepared for a training program which can very much help in the fast economic growth and development.

Now let us see how this laymn class contributes to its Economy. A survey report has been prepared on case studies of following people:

FROM PROD UCTION TO CONSUMPTION

Me and My Economy

A Farmer's Economy

Case Study of a Farmer

I am a small farmer. In this modern age of science and technology, I am still dependent on the natural means of cultivation and irrigation. 'As you sow you shall reap' does not go with me because what I sow, depends on rains. I may and may not reap the same. Sometimes draughts, sometimes floods, sometimes poor market conditions, sometimes corrupt middlemen, all such conditions are the real hazards in my economic growth and development. But even then I have heard of the Green Revolution in India. Therefore I have heard of the improvement in the quality and quantity of Indias, agricultural production. I do not have modern means of irrigation. I am still looking at the sky for the success or failure of my crops. I cannot afford to buy good quality seeds, good pesticides, good storage facilities, good markets, etc.

Thus we see that a small farmer's economy depends on luck and chance and not on the technical advancement which has taken place in Indian agriculture.

India is a land of rich resources, the second most populous country of the world, and the fifth largest nation of the world in its area, and it is an agricultural economy. Therefore, the policies of the Government should be formulated in such a manner that small farmers may also get economic justice. Higher loan facilities should be made available to them and a well planned training program should also be provided.

Me and My Economy

A Laborer's Economy

Case Study of a Laborer

I am a small laborer. But the industrialisation of economies is made possible not by machineries only,; my skilled form has also played a major role. Either I am working on a farm land or in an industry, my economy depends on the economic behavior of my owner. Industrialisation is a field of economics that studies the strategic behavior of firms, the structure of markets and their interactions. The success of an industry depends on the conduct of its firms and the success of a firm depends on the conduct of its laborers.

At the small scale level of an economy, the laborers are the main factors of production, whereas at the large scale level, the skilled labor can only manage the modern techniques. But a laborer's economy is always exploited by the big industries and big industrialists. Hand-made goods are always beaten up by the machine-made goods. The economies with higher population should always opt for labor-intensive techniques, but to compete with international markets, the highly populated economies also give preference to capital-intensive techniques. Therefore, labor do not get economic justice. It is because the major part of the profits are enjoyed by the big industrialists. This exploitation of one class by another leads to strikes, violence, and other anti-social acts.

Thus for the all-round development of an economy, this discrimination between classes should be avoided and such policies should be formulated that no class conflict should harm any economy. In addition, the fruits of economic growth should not be eaten only by a part of the population. Here the role of economic justice need to be given the highest importance.

In an economy where there is no political stability, and law and order are in bad shape, there that economy needs revolutionary changes.

An efficient, hardworking, disciplined, honest, and a well wisher of all type of owner gives rise to his laborers by giving them finance and facilities both, whereas an inefficient, dishonest owner exploits his laborers by giving them low wages and no other facilities. This type of owner can give rise to himself only and not to his society, economy or nation. For his personal profit-maximization, he misuses his power and they work only for his own benefits and selfish motives.

Though modern technologies have replaced my role but it is partial only. Still the industrial and agricultural development of any economy is based on my efforts. In small scale industries, we small laborers or are the main factors of production and in large scale industries we manage the modern techniques. All present day machineries are run by skilled labor but unfortunately, we are exploited by the big industrialists. Moreover, our hand-made goods are also beaten up by the machine-made goods. Therefore, in such economics where population is higher, the industrialists should use labor-intensive techniques in their vast areas. So I being a small laborer, do not get economic justice. It is because the major part of profits of my economy is enjoyed by the big industrialist or big agriculturist only. This exploitation of one class by another class leads to class-conflict. And this class-conflict leads to strikes, unrest and violence. Thus for economic growth, and development economic justice is essential.

In developing economies, if law and order are in bad shape, a corrupt class-imerges, a class of middlemen. Then, under the name of democracy, we see the bureaucracy and the democratic values, national values, patriotic values, social values, moral values replaced by cut-throat values, selfish values, terrorist values, violent values, inhuman values. Therefore, this type of economic system needs a change. From production to consumption a long chain of people works and these people are from different parts of a city, called a socio-economic structure. As an economy grows, its socio-economic structure also changes with the advanced technology and improvement in the quantity and quality of production and education and more and more people grow from lower standards to higher, socio-economic standards. But due to unequal distribution of income, the disparity between higher class and lower class increases.

Therefore, if we wish to improve our economy, we must take such steps to reduce this disparity or inequality of income in all the economies of the whole world.

In India, the corrupt politicians are playing the game of Economy-Economy. It is because 60% of them perhaps did not study the subject of economics at all. They don't know what economics is? That's why this scientific subject has becomes a tool in their hands with which they are playing the game of Economy-Economy. Whosoever is the elected leader, owns the economy and economic powers and thinks that he has the full right to play with his economy. As the election term is for five years only, so such people in the fear that they may not be elected in the next term, and they misuse their economic power for their selfish motives only. So a stable political position is needed, which should be patriotic, devoted, sincere, honest and be based on humanity and human values for a rapid rise in its economy.

2

Meaning and Definitions of Economics

Economics may be defined in many ways.

Economics is a social - science that seeks to analyze and describe the production, distribution and consumption of wealth.

Economics is the study of mankind, in the ordinary business of life. It is a science which studies human beings economic behavior.

Economics is the study of how individuals and societies choose to employ those resources for taking decision about what goods and services will be produced, how will be produced, and for whom to be produced.

Economics may be the future or cornerstone upon which we rely even in terms of setting our personal values and mores, power, family life, education and social consciousness may all one day be based on economics.

Economics helps us to understand societal and global affairs, helps us to become better informed voters, and teach us about choice and decision-making.

Economics is often defined as a body of knowledge or study that discusses how a society tries to solve the human problems of unlimited wants and scarce resources, because economics is associated with human behavior.

Economics is a game theory which is concerned with the situation in which several decision-makers interact in the sense that the degree of satisfaction achieved by anyone of them depends not only on his or her choices, but also on the choices made by all the players.

So these are some of the definitions of eEconomics.

Economics is such an important subject which each and every individual of an economy must be familiar with. As every child matters for a school, in the same way every individual matters for an economy. Whether we are a student of economics or not, whether we are studying economics as a subject or not, we all must know what economics is and how we all should nourish our economy, and how we all should work for the growth of our economy. An economy means a system which provides us work as per our efficiency, and pays us money for the work we have done for it.

From the Mouth of An Economy

Yes, I am an Economy. Let me introduce myself to you. When Money was not in existence, I was known as Barter Economy. At that time people used to satisfy their needs by exchanging goods and services with each other. I was very simple and the level of satisfaction among people was very high. But now, as much as I am progressing, I am known as Money Economy, I have become very complicated; modernization, advanced technology and scientific methods have changed me totally. A layman doesn't know about these. I have become a concern of only that proportion of population who are known as economists, administrators, politicians, scientists, entrepreneurs, industrialists, agriculturist,

All these classes, who know me very well, they also exploit me very well. All these classes are standing on the shoulders of a huge class known as a class of laymen who doesn't know -What economics is?

Today I will explain to you my meaning.

Come on **'Lets Play Economy-Economy.'**

It is very interesting and a very useful game.

The very first lesson of this game is that we all have to nourish our economy by putting the best of our efforts. If we learn only to Exploit economy, then we cannot do justice with our economy. And for a fair game the feeling of nourishing should overpower the feeling of exploitation.

Economy is a system and each and every individual is a part of this System and all individuals are equally important for me. Even beggers are a part of my system. If you learn only a single lesson of nourishing your economy, you will not find a single begger on this earth. There will be no class called Poor on this earth. This is all happening because a few so called upper classes are exploting me.

So it is very important that all individuals should know the meaning of Economics. After knowing this meaning, you will have better understanding of casting your precious vote. Nobody will dare to buy you for a little amount of money. You give your economy in the hands of such people who exploit me only for a few selfish purposes and not for the betterment of economy as a whole.

If only a few sectors are improving, I do not call it economic growth.

3

Let's Play Economy-Economy

This chapter "Let's Play Economy-Economy' has threefold aims.

It is aimed at bringing awareness to each and every individual to know the word Economy. As it is very very important for an individual to know his/her place in its Economy and the importance of their economic Behavior to shape up their economy, to think seriously and sincerely about his/ her important role in their economy. Whether he/she is contributing physical labor or mental labor, that should not matter, without any discrimination of the type of labor they are putting in their economy, only that is important. And this deep understanding of the word Economy will make them understand how valuable they are for their economy. It is their own economy. The feeling of ownership of economy will help them at the time of casting their vote, they will not hand over their economy in the hands of corrupt and selfish leaders. After knowing their importance for their economy they will not make wrong decisions at the time of elections, they will not sell their vote for suffering in the long run.

Indian economy is suffering from this serious disease of unawareness. If people are made aware through properly planned training programs for all sectors of economy, then the economy may restructure and reshape itself for its alround development. Being an over populated country, it needs its research and technological development to work out in the field of labor-intensive techniques, whereas the modern trend is towards the capital-intensive techniques. Capitalist countries search markets for their final goods and agricultural economies are their targets to get raw material for their modern machineries .With globalisation their chances became more bright and the results are there that Indian goods cannot compete with them, which leads to decline in demand for our products. Therefore, we need the same old simple Indian agricultural economy when the level of satisfaction was very high among our masses. Now in this complicated age of tough competition, everything has changed. With this competitive progress, the real economic growth is not achieved, the level of real satisfaction has also gone down. The value of Indian money in international markets is continuously declining. We are facing serious worldwide recession's repercussions on our economy under the heavy pressure of international debt. But to fool ourselves we have a fake smile on our faces by keeping our eyes closed like the pigeon before the big cat of capitalist economies by thinking all is well.

Thus there is need to recollect ourselves, to be an alround developed economy we need to bring awareness of real economic growth. Real Economy Growth can take place only when we take Real Right Decisions. We should stop running the blind race with the capitalist countries, otherwise in the long run, our coming generations must be prepared to face the adverse results of today's prevailing recessions in all the sectors of our economy.

Therefore, each and every individual, in whatsoever sector of economy, he/she is working, should learn to nourish their economy by their sincere efforts. For this we need training schedules for the whole working force of our economy.

Secondly, this book is aimed at realizing the importance of the subject Economics as an independent stream and must be introduced from the primary standard onwards by the name of economics only and not as a part of social science. It is because economics is a very natural scientific subject which is related with our heart and home. It starts automatically with our birth, our economic behaviour begins before any other behaviour. A child at the time of birth starts its demand for milk, clothes, medicines etc. etc. So when the child grows up, we need to tell him/her that it is their economic behavior which is different from economic activity.

Therefore, the subject Economics must be introduced in a playway method, by making the classroom a mini economy and with a nice game 'Lets Play Economy - Economy" The following projects may be displayed in all the class-rooms of a school. For example, in fifth standard the class room project of an economy may be displayed as

"The Project of an Economy with its all Factors of Production"

Land, Labor's Capital' Entrepreneur

In sixth standard it may be termed as -

The project of Physical Shape of an Economy

Schools, Colleges, Industries, Hotels, Offices, Farms, Shops, Corporates, etc., etc.

In the seventh standard the project may be termed as -

"Project of an Economy with its Major Sectors"

Primary sector Agriculture and other related activities, secondary sector industries and other related activities, tertiary sector-Services and the other related activities

In the eighth standard

Project of the Role of Financial Markets in an Economy

Likewise for ninth standard

Project on the Rest of the world in an Economy

For tenth standard -

Project of Comparison between Developed and Developing Economies

The eleventh and twelfth standards may run as they are running with CBSE syllabus; and that is, Indian Economics and Statistics in the eleventh and in twelfth Micro and Macro Economics.

Thus in early childhood itself the students will become aware of the subject of Economics and will realize their importance for their economy. Becoming aware and thinking seriously and sincerely may definitely change the pattern of an Economy. And today, though the status of Indian economy for international consumer market may be high as India is the best market for them and for their foreign goods, but what about our own domestic products? Definitely their demand is reducing.

Therefore, with the increasing importance of the subject of Economics, the economy will reshape itself. As Economic Growth and Education go together, more education leads to faster economic growth. The investments in education could pay for themselves in the long run, and could also play a role in reducing poverty. Such reasoning could be crucial in bolstering political support for educational investments and ensuring their sustainability. There is need balancing education and training system is in developing countries. In addition, vocational education may also help in preparing out of school youth for livelihood. Technical and vocational education and training has already fueled phenomenal economic growth in many countries. Access to education is one of the highest priorities on the development agenda of developing economies.

The third aim of this book is to give a message to our masses that whatsoever role we are playing to keep up our economy, we should learn to nourish our economy and not to exploit it for our selfish motives.

The corrupt leaders who are playing with the economy, should stop this game of playing Economy-Economy. They should undergo a well planned training module from time to time. It is essential because in this age of Education, we have many uneducated leaders also among us. A minimum qualification must be kept under rules and regulations. And those who are uneducated and running the country, must undergo a training program for better understanding of their economy.

The meaning of Real Economic Growth must be understood by our current leaders. It must be explained to them through training modules, without which no leader can be a successful leader and no economy can be an economy with alround growth and development. If only a few sectors or only one portion of the population progresses, that doesn't mean real economic growth. The real economic growth can be attained only if each and every individual of the economy enjoys the fruits of economic development.

Thus I have included Training Programs for all sectors of an Economy in this book. It is because Education is no use if it is not revived with the help of Training as per the demand of the fast changing conditions. So for Economy as a whole, each and every sector has to have continuous progress.

Let's Play Economy—Economy

I am an Economy. My all individuals, whether they have studied economics or not, whether they know any definition of Economics or not, all are equally important for me. Each and every individual contributes to its Economy.

Therefore, you all should be aware of the meaning of Economics. It is defined by a huge number of economists but today a layman will tell you my meaning.

According to a layman an economy is a system which provides us work and for doing that work we get money to satisfy our needs. When money was not in existence, I was known as Barter economy. All people used to exchange goods with each other, the economy was very simple, but the level of satisfaction was very high. Now my picture is very complicated and the level of satisfaction is very poor.

As it is important that all individuals should know the meaning of an Economy, similarly, it is also very important that all should know that how should we nourish our economy.

If we all work for our economy, and not only for self interest, then perhaps there won't be any poor economy on this earth. As the educational system, educational policies have so much in them to improve the social behavior, moral behavior, political behavior of it's masses, what is being done till now to improve the economic behavior of its economy?

If we all learn to nourish our economy, then this world economy will never face the type of recession it is facing today. Why does this type of Recession occur in the economy? The answer is very straightforward and that is as follows—

It is because—

1. The production is effective but the distribution is defective.
2. The Economic Powers are effective but the Political Powers are defective.
3. The Human Power is effective but Humanity is defective.
4. The Policies are effective but the Applications are defective.
5. Economic Laws are effective but unstable Political Laws are defective.
6. Politics is effective but Politicians are defective
7. Systems are effective but Approaches are defective.
8. Past Culture is effective but Present Culture is defective.
9. Modernization is effective but Media is defective.
10. Spiritual Power is effective but Religious Power is defective.

11. Creater is effective but Creatures are defective.

Therefore to Nourish our respective economies, we all should know our individual role and its importance, then only we can overcome our defects and recessions.

We should start this game - Lets Play Economy-Economy - in each and every school so that each and every child will learn the practical meaning of Economics.

Economics is the subject which is very close to Heart and Home. It is because the economic behavior of an individual starts at first before its social behavior and any other of its personality behavior. Its demand starts from its birth. The child's economic behavior speaks and shows that the child knows the meaning of Utility and Satisfaction. The need is only to specify that this is your Economic Behavior.

So if an individual learns from its childhood about Economics, he or she will not only know to exploit its economy for personal interests but they will learn to know the ways of nourishing their economy also.

So come on- Let's Play Economy-Economy

1. A Farmer's Economy vs an Agriculturist's Economy
2. A Laborer's Economy vs an Industrialist's Economy
3. A Leader's Economy vs a Politicians' Economy
4. A Soldier's Economy vs an Army Officer's Economy
5. A Lawyer's Economy vs a Judge's Economy
6. A Firm's Economy vs an Industrialist's Economy
7. A Policeman's Economy vs a DCP's Economy

8. An Educationist's Economy vs an Economist's Economy
9. A Doctor's Economy vs a Hospital's Economy.
10. A Voter's Economy vs a Country's Economy.

A Full-fledged economy is comprised of all above mentioned parts of an economy. Now if all these parts of an economy playa fair game by not only exploiting their economy for their self -development, but also develop their economy as a whole, then we can see a picture of A Happy World Economy.

The following steps may be taken for **A Happy World Economy:**

1. By remodeling our schools.
2. By in-service training programs for all sectors of an economy.
3. By in-service training of all government officials.
4. By in-service training of all uneducated but elected members of Parliament.
5. By establishing training and development agencies with the help of out standing educationists, educational consultants and retired experienced personnel.
6. By the help of extended services to achieve the goal of Every Individual Matter. (EIM)
7. By the Economy Improvement Planning Framework (EIPF)
   a) Where you are?
   b) What do you want to accomplish?
   c) A clear idea of how the framework can help?
8. By constitutional changes for equal importance to all sectors and individuals.

4

Economics Education in Indian Schools

As Economics is a very important subject for each and every individual to know about it because Economics may be the future cornerstone upon which we rely even in terms of setting our personal values and mores, power, family life, education; and social consciousness may all one day be based on Economics.

Economics improves individuals and gives them better understanding for societal and global affairs. It teaches us about choice and decision-making.

As each and every factor of production is part and parcel of its economy, so each and every person should know its accurate role and contribution to the growth and development of its economy.

It is a general ideology that only policy-makers should know about the economic tools to run the economy smoothly, whereas each and every individual should have the knowledge of economic tools. For example a businessman who has never studied the subject of economics but it reflects in his economic behavior. He understands automatically the processes of production, distribution, consumption, savings, investments, price-policy, monetary policy, banking procedures, etc. etc.

Unfortunately in Indian schools economics is introduced after tenth standard only as a full fledged subject. Before that it is known as only a social science subject where as economics education should be introduced as a separate stream. Economics is the study of mankind in the ordinary business of life. It is a science which studies human beings economic behavior.

Economic modernization is a remedy for all social ills or difficulties. Schools can be very economically important to countries. Economic growth and development of each and every country depends on the economic behavior of its masses which is the major resource especially in highly populated countries. Schools may be used as mini economies to make the students understand from their early age that the real growth is the growth of all the sectors of an economy, If only a few sectors of an economy develop, that may not be considered as economic growth. An economy needs to grow as a whole.

In schools we may develop several economic modules for all classes separately. Through these modules the meaning of Economics can be understood by the students in a playway method. The school is the largest and most appropriate unit for imparting the knowledge and making solid base for any subject which has practical utility for an individual for his whole life. Economics is the subject which is very useful for all. Therefore, all classes from the fourth standard onwards must be familiar with the word Economy. In the fourth class the economic module should be based only on the working of the parents, as the child knows about the working of his/her parents. The need is only to tell them that your parents are very important for the Economy because they are contributing in its production. Then the whole class may be termed as a mini economy and children may be asked to choose a profession for them and the class should play Economy-Economy.

In this way all the classes should be given different modules to play Economy-Economy. All of a sudden when students are introduced with the term Economics, and that too with a bundle of difficult definitions without understanding the meaning of Economics, then this very owned subject which is very natural, scientific, very near to home and heart for its economic behavior, becomes a strange subject for students. Therefore, Economics education is in the need to get its importance at the initial stage of education and should be introduced as a separate stream after the tenth standard.

5

How Can We Nourish Our Economy

Economy is an integral part of everyone and everybody is an integral part of its Economy. Then how can we do without thinking of its nourishing. Everyone of us knows about exploiting its resources to obtain maximum satisfaction, similarly, we all should know about nourishing our Economy.

In the production process of an economy, we all produce either goods or services. But if the produced goods and services does not undergo a justified distribution process then that economy does not get nourishment.

An economy is nourished only when all the sectors of an economy grow equally: when the fruits of economic growth are distributed equally to all individuals, either he is a small farmer or a big agriculturist, either he is a small labourer or a big industrialist.

The study of Economics is aimed at enabling individuals to carry out activities related to goods and services in such a manner that optimum benefit is obtained from the activity. It is a study of production processes, distribution processes, consumption patterns and human behavior during all these processes. The aim is to devise the most effective way of functioning.

There are various economic systems such as the Capitalistic system, Socialistic system, Communistic system or Mixed Economic system. The economists of a country function as per the guidelines of the prevailing economic system in that country.

It is time we reclaim the original idea that making responsible choices to integrate smart economics is very important in the 21st century. India is an agricultural economy but sadly, this sector is always taken for granted. 70% of Indias population participates in agriculture and is responsible for 30% of our G.D.P. Despite significant increases in agricultural growth rates; it not making a direct and proportional impact on the G.D.P.

It is a well known fact that the growth of the agricultural sector has an indirect but incremental effect on all the other sectors of our economy. The tenth five-year plan (2002-2007) envisaged a 4% growth in the agriculture sector. Though the impact on GD.P. would be less than a percentage point, the gain for other sectors would be immense.

The agricultural sector not only ensures food security for the nation, but also assures livelihood security for millions. Therefore, for an agricultural economy it is essential that prime importance should be given to agricultural sector.

Other important factors for nourishing an economy are as under.

1. Political Stability

To nourish an economy political stability is essential. It is because political instability gives rise to corruption.

If an economy is politically stable, its economic growth and development may be seen in all sectors of that economy. Generally, in democratic countries the election tenure is for five years and if the elected people are not honest, they do not use the public money for people's welfare, they misuse it under the fear that after five years they may and may not be elected. Therefore, for the nourishment of an economy and to improve its economic condition, it is necessary that it should have a stable and viable government because it is the government only who formulates all the economic policies. The important economic policies are: Price-Policy, Trade-Policy, Employment-Policy, Tax-Policy, Monetary-Policy, Fiscal-Policy, Production-Policy, Consumption- Policy, Distribution-Policy, etc., etc.

Thus for all round economic growth and development, the role of government is very important. It is observed that economies with stable and strong political conditions rise very fast as compared to the economies with unstable political conditions.

Economic development is the increase in the standard of living of a nation's population, with sustained growth from a simple low income economy to a modern high income economy. An economy's economic, political and social conditions are inter-related with each other.

2. Removal of all types of inequalities.
3. Children should by owned by the Government after the age of ten years and providing good quality of life to them based on hard work, discipline and sacrifice.
4. Moral education, to be the part and parcel of all disciplines of education.

5. A very strong check on media for not showing violence, passion and nudity
6. Continues training programs for the law and order sector of the economy.
7. By putting checks on the commercialisation of education by giving the educational services neither to government nor to private hands, but to a class of social-workers, which should include retired persons from all the sectors of an economy, not for profit-maximisation but only for the growth and development of an economy.

⑥

How to Attain Economic Justice

Economic justice touches the individual person as well as the social order, which encompasses the moral principles which guide us in designing our economic institutions. These institutions determine how each person earns a living, enters into contracts, exchanges goods and services with others and otherwise produces independently.

Economic justice may be defined within two parameters:

1. To each according to one's needs;
2. To each according to one's contribution.

Now to maintain social order, economic justice may be achieved by the intervention of government for determining the just price, the just wages and the just profit.

Distributive justice follows participative justice and breaks down income-producing income when all persons are not given equal opportunity to acquire and enjoy the fruits of income-producing property. Therefore, the principle of harmony encompasses the balancing principles required to detect distortions of either the input or output principles and to make whatever corrections are needed to restore a just and balanced economic order for all.

Mixed Economogy as Modern economy

Today most of the modern economies are based on the principles of mixed economy. In a mixed type economy both the private ownership as well as the state takes part in the means of production, distribution and other types of economic activities.

The mixed economy allows private participation in the field of production in an environment of competition with an objective of attaining profit. On the contrary following, the features of Socialism it includes public ownership in production for maximizing social welfare. In other words, in mixed economy all economic activities are decided by the government as well as by private owners. A system based on sovereignty of each person within institutions embodying principles of social justice.

Is economic justice the name of a virtue or a principle?

Aristotle deals chiefly with Justice as a particular virtue found in special contexts, not as a foundation principle of society. It is discussed as courage or liberality or temperateness. The contexts are three: (1) distribution, (2) correction, and (3) reciprocal exchange. Now the principles derived from the virtue in each context depends on the kind of society.

The present economic world order represented by globalization and laissez faire economy, is the path leading to global economic avation.

Indian government decides to accelerate the rate of economic growth and to speed up indutrialization, to develop heavy industries, to reduce disparities in income and wealth through economic reform and social justice. Some implications are the timing of the various policies and their sequencing and the relative importance attached to the different aspects of policy, relating to the provision of education, health and employment, globalization of the economy and encourage economic development.

7

Professional Development

Professional development refers to the development of an individual in his/her professional role. For all professionals in any field, new opportunities for growth, exploration, learning and development are always welcome. Professional development includes formal experiences (FE) and informal experiences (IE). FE includes attending workshops, attending seminars and meetings, monitoring or learning through mentors. IE includes referring to and reading professional publications, learning through TV programs, watching documentaries related to different academic disciplines.

Professional development (PD) is a broader term than career development (CD). CD is defined as the growth that occurs as he/she moves through the professional career cycle. Whereas PD examines the content of experiences and processes by which the professional development will occur and the contexts in which it will take place. PD is a concept which processes in long term and includes regular opportunities as well as experiences, planned systematically to promote growth and development in the profession.

In this century of advancement of science and technology, all national and international organizations have supported and acknowledged the importance of PD. They have supported the implementation of all those initiatives which aimed at improving the professional skills and knowledge of professionals of all sectors of economy. It favours the concept of lifelong learning. To relate prior knowledge to new experiences and a regular follow up support, is regarded as an indispensable catalyst of the changing process.

The Agencies of PD

The role of the agencies of PD is very caring. PD is meant to aid the professionals in building new pedagogical theories and practices and to help them to develop their expertise in their respective fields. PD takes place either as a collaborative process or as an isolated work and reflection. But the more effective way for PD to occur, may be seen when there are meaningful and reasonably necessary interactions take place not only among the professionals themselves but also between professionals, administrators and other officials working in that particular field. The processes and technologies of PD has to be considered within a framework of social, economic and political trends and events.

The purpose of PD is to teach and train people, how to become lifelong learners and virtuous human beings to build up the capacity to adapt to the drastically changing values, and to become masters of faster changing technologies.

Professional Training for Secondary Sector and Career Development

To help and address the needs of secondary sector continued PD is needed to support professionals who are already in the work force to increase the awareness of new technologies and support the development of the marketable skills sets in a wide variety of employment settings. Expanding technically advanced skills in commercial systems that affect the energy to work and good working conditions is necessary to support the changing needs of today's industries. Professionals and fully qualified work-force leads to fast economic growth.

Reshaping the Professionals

Secondary sector includes both, the public bodies as well as private bodies. The most important reform introduced recently of inducing foreign investment has changed the face of Indian economy. Indian economy is providing complete security to foreign investors. With this change now Indian economy as a mixed economy is emerging as a most powerful market of the world. But at the same time we should not forget that inducement of foreign investment may harm our industrial growth and development in the long run. Specially small scale industries and handicraft industries might face hard competition.

The present situation of Indian economy is that the process of structural changes has contributed to observed changes in factor shares, that is, the share of labour has increased and that of land and capital has decreased. India has become the second largest GDP among new emerging economies based on PPP (Purchasing Power Parity). Since independence India has achieved self-sufficiency in manufacturing a variety of basic and capital goods. Indian industrial growth with an equitable international economic order can be much more stronger if professional development or skill development of the whole secondary sector is given importance not only at state level but also at national level.

To ensure growth and development, self-reliance, modernization and social justice, professional development is very important in the secondary sector. The power, transport and other infrastructural industries are owned by the state governments railways, road transport, shipping, aviation, oils, telecommunications, research and development activities etc. are supported by the government at the centre. The public sector as well as private sector both are showing performance of the Indian economy in the world market.

There is a great need for promoting an industrial environment where the acquisition of advanced technological capability receives priority. In this world of modern technological changes, the relationship between the technology-provider and the supplier of technology must be a continuous process. Now if the government induces professional training for private as well as public, both the sectors, it will strengthen them. Government will also improve those enterprises which fall in the reserved areas of operation or are in high priority areas or are generating goods at reasonable profit with the growing complexity of industrial structure

Thus with the growing complexity of Industrial structure and for ensuring high productivity and *to* compete in the international market the professional training or professional development must take place in the economy.

Professional Development in Tertiary Sector

Continued professional training is always needed *to* support professionals already in the working force.

Skill development is very important in education sector. Education leads to faster economic growth. It plays a very important role in reducing poverty. But as education yields slow returns it does not get the political support whereas the importance of Education makes its place in developing economies. Balancing education and training systems in modern economies has become an important issue for any type of economic system.

Vocational Education is also one of very important stream of education which includes youth livelihood toolkit. It goes with the theme of Earning while Learning. Technical and vocational education and training has fueled the phenomena of economic growth in some countries and fallen short of expectations in some others. To increase and improve the quality of education, improvement in the management of teachers is very important Access to education or education for all is the main agenda of every developing nation. For good economic growth and good quality of education, better incentives for students and teachers are very necessary.

Professional development in services sector includes development of abilities and capacities of local government officials, planners, citizens' task force groups, architects, engineers, designers, working force of health dept., safety and welfare dept., etc., etc.

As the services sector is growing continuously and becoming more significant in every economic structure, the professional services are expected to improve its performance both domestically and globally.

Professional training to services sector is known as in-service training. The reshaping of professionals is very necessary to compete in international market. Though the contribution of the professional services to

GDP is relatively smaller than primary and secondary sector, even then we cannot underestimate the importance of this sector in nation-building. The group of services included are accountancy, legal, engineering, medical and similar other services. The business models adopted by professional services may determine the quality of services offered and their level of competitiveness. These professional units are limited in terms of their brain power, intellectual assets, and financial capabilities. For a high income economy we need high quality of professional services in the highly competitive global markets. The study of human resource development and its excellent management has reached today to its highest level and the process of acquiring knowledge in this field has become multi-dimensional. For all professionals in any field, new opportunities for growth, exploration, learning and development are all lifelong processes to achieve with excellence. It is based on constructivism and it is long term process. The professional training of services sector deals with the goals, objectives and purposes of professional development and the context in which professional development has to take place.

8

In-service Training Programes for all Sectors of Economy

Economic progress is directly related to in-service programs for all sectors of an economy. Training means improving and not doing only the routine work. Or training means thinking more, doing more, improving more, putting more and more efforts to improve your working and above all achieving more and again more.

For each and every sector of the economy, there is need of a well planned training program.

1. Training Programs for Agriculture and other related activities.
2. Training Programs for Industries and other related activities.
3. Training Programs for Services sector.

Objective of Training for all Sectors of an Economy

The purpose of training or education is to train people to get jobs or to be self employed. The importance of professional training and overall educational attainment is increasing in all developing nations. It should be based on constructivism rather than on transmission.

1. Improvement of personal skills

2. Improving or upgrading competences and working capabilities.
3. Raising the achievement level
4. Keeping abreast of current technologies and developments.
5. Developing positive attitudes and values with changing new ideologies
6. Developing faith in and respect for work.
7. Team-building spirit to be developed for fair division of work.
8. Motivating
9. Developing abilities to make decisions
10. Learning for guiding, delegating and evaluating
11. Learning management

Professional Training for Agricultural Sector

As India is an agricultural economy, but due to unfavourable farm prospects and no access to subsidies, work in the same direction has led to a negative attitude towards farming. The importance of professional training cannot be overemphasized in the process of a shrinking farm sector and a non-farm sector that becomes more decisive for rural livelihood. An exit from farming becomes more probable if the farm is located closer to an urban centre. However, a significant share of farm families plans to take steps towards diversification and non-farm incomes. And once they leave this sector, they never want to return back to farming again.

There is a trend of hobby farming also, so even if the subsistence farming disappears gradually, hobby farming processes would keep the small farms alive.

Thus small farms due to lack of any professional training, fear the prospect of becoming uncompetitive in the open markets for their small scale farming structure. Therefore, government should make structural policies at the heart of sector-related policies.

If the government through professional training and education in farming and non-farming sector takes initiatives then perhaps migration trend from rural to urban sectors will be reduced. Nevertheless, professional training and education is very important for the non-farm sector. Though the government or banks are introducing many more credit schemes to the farmers they hardly approach to the capital credit markets. It is because they themselves are reluctant to take credit and the fear of nonpayment of credit due to crop failure also bothers them. But at the same time access to credit markets by farmers is essential for structural adjustments. If the credit schemes are not designed properly, it may become a burden on the budget of people.

Hence, it is necessary to provide professional training and apart from sectoral policies for agriculture and agro-food processing with other non-farm subsistence activities, policies addressing the whole rural sector are very important for sustainable rural development.

Small farmers constitute a major portion of population. Farming can provide a prosperous future to small farmers if they develop within by obtaining professional training for improving their small farms .And when they will get higher returns from small farms, they will stop migrating to urban areas.

9

Education and Training Modules with School-Based In-service Teachers' Training Modules

Learning reform is at the heart of education reform as well as teachers and plays a significant role in developing the quality of learners.

It is therefore essential for the development of individual teachers to be able to reform the learning process in accordance with the requirements of the knowledge-based society in order to improve the quality of learners or students to their full potential.

The training programmes for developing in-service teachers in Delhi schools have been mainly organized by the S.C.E.R.T. which involves high expenditures; and most of the training uses lectures more than practice and closes without monitoring or evaluating the training program.

This type of training is a one short affair which has no continuity. Therefore a new method of in-service teachers training is required which should be effective and sustainable and should take place at the school itself.

The office of the Education Councilor of the National Education Commission following the law related to reorganization of the ministry of education, which should be a government agency responsible for educational policy and planning should launch projects on teacher development to study an effective training for development in-service teachers.

The results of the study will reveal that school-based training (SBT) is a new paradigm to develop the teachers and the teaching profession as well as to contribute to the success of the learning reform in Delhi schools. The priority for teacher development should be school-based in-service teacher training.

The SBT plan will recommend various strategies including that for development of teachers' capacity which could be enhanced through SBT.

Study and Results

The four pilot projects of the Education Council will be as follows:

1. **Master Learner Project:** This project is aimed at selecting outstanding teachers who are able to use the student-centered approach for the learning process of their students. Those selected master learners will receive a subsidy per person to create hundred teachers network during four months to adopt the student-centered approach. This network of Master-Learners will keep on increasing year by year.
2. **National Learner Project**: This project is aimed at selecting outstanding teachers who are able to conduct research and development on learning reform. Those selected teachers will be recognized as National Learners. They will receive a subsidy per person to conduct a research and development as well as to train a network of fellow teachers during his/her research for two years. These National Learners will train this network of teachers to adopt the student-centered-approach.

3. **Master Learners and National Learners**: The Training by Learning Reform Agents such as Master Learners and National Learners can help other teachers in schools to change their behavior of traditional teaching into Student-centered-approach. This teachers network at schools will be termed as KalyanKari Model Prashikshan Welfare Model It will focus on training at school and meeting the needs of the teachers.
4. **Project on Research and Development on Models of School-Based Training** - The objective is to develop model of SBT. as well as to make teachers appreciated and be able to adopt the student-centered-approach for their teaching and learning process. The office of Education Council will select ten teaching profession societies/associations and will provide them with financial support to conduct research and training on SBT models. The participatory processes will show new innovation teacher development. The students will learn happily and enjoy themselves so much doing many activities to seek gain and knowledge by themselves. Moreover, SBT models need only small amounts of money to use for Necessary expenses.
5. **Project to Support School-Based Training:** Policy and strategic plan for in-service teacher development for the promotion of learning reform—The objective of this module is to select the agent teachers to train their fellow teachers. The principals of schools would be instructed that they should recognize, support and facilitate all the training program. The teachers trainers themselves should be accepted and regarded as leaders of learning reforms.

10

Objectives of SBIT for In-service Teachers' Development

The objectives are, to—

1. Improve or upgrade competences and working capabilities of teachers and learners.
2. Help teachers and learners to identify and solve problems faced in and outside the school.
3. Provide on-the-job training in other aspects of teaching profession.
4. Raise the achievement level of pupils.
5. Reduce drop-outs/repeaters.
6. Keep abreast of new developments in education for own advancement and professional development.
7. Meet requirements of curriculum change.
8. Induce/orient new teachers to perform their jobs properly.
9. Help teachers to identify and solve their own and pupils' problems.
10. Help educational personnel to identify the training needs of teachers.
11. Develop positive attitudes and values among teachers to improve the teaching learning process.

12. Encourage teachers to take an active role in improving and planning and evaluating educational programs in their schools and community.
13. Enrich teachers' experience in view of individual advancement of their profession.
14. Better teachers' understanding of the teaching profession.
15. Evolve suggestions for developing an effective in-service programme.
16. Reviewing the curriculum and text -books.
17. Analyze institutional objectives.
18. Develop skills in developing content units and teaching modes and other related teaching materials.
19. Develop techniques in assessing the students' achievements.
20. Develop skills by collecting and utilizing locally available resources in teaching.
21. Develop a positive attitude towards activity-based integrated teaching methodology.
22. Develop interest in action-research and develop faith in and respect for work.
23. Help in altering children's behavior and strategies of developing their personality.
24. Develop teachers' awareness of role and responsibility in SBIT.
25. Make use of SBIT to support national development goals.

Thus due to technological changes in in-service training is inevitable and cannot be ignored in educational improvement effort. Often in-service education has been attended to as a type of training addressed to teachers, but usually prepared by outside agencies or central offices. This has happened in the past because traditionally in-service education has been the responsibility of experts or specialists and therefore, planned and implemented by them. This process has, however, been found expensive and often unrelated to the actual needs of the teachers. It takes the teacher out of the class-room. Teachers receive some personal benefit but a very little benefit for their school and students.

Ten Key Factors - Required for SBIT Module

1. Principals/school administrators will provide the necessary support and encouragement as well as facilitate the training to achieve the desired goals. They should see to it that the teacher development plan forms a part of the annual school-work plan. They also assist in obtaining additional resources required for the whole school reform.
2. Training Organizers — They are a group of teachers who fully appreciate the needs for training of teachers and are cognizant with the various problems encountered. They collectively conceptualize the training through identifying the goals and objectives bearing in mind the actual situations and the needs of the teachers as well as the school. They also serve as trainers in some cases.
3. Trainers — Trainers are the teachers endowed with knowledge and outstanding capability of applying the learner-centered approach required for education reform. Being knowledgeable, creative and with expertise in teachers' development, they will be accepted and win the respect of their peers.

4. Trainees — Trainees are those who are genuinely interested and volunteer to receive training.
5. Training-Period — It is at the direction of the organizers and the trainers. The training, however, should be long- term and be on a regular basis and continued until achievement of the desired objectives. The training schedule should be flexible and an activity can be organized on the hour/day suitable to trainers and trainees alike during the holidays, in the morning before the class begins, after lunch or after the class.
6. Training Content — It depends on the needs of the school and the trainees. However, it should meet the National Educational Guidelines following National Educational Act which focuses on learning reform.
7. Training Venue — The training will take place in the school or even in the class-room itself for authentic situation; suitable learning sources in the community of the school could also be availed of.
8. Budgetary Requirement — The necessary budget for teachers' development should be included in the annual school work plan. Teachers under training must be provided a subsidy for self-development.
9. Evaluation — It will be made before and after the training.
10. Training Model — The trainers will use the SBIT models which will comprised PDCA model.

11

Model of SBT School-Based Training

Process Methodology: an overview - 1 Practitioner

No teacher comes out of the teacher-training institute as a fullfledged teacher. Hence, there will always be a need for in-service education programmes for teachers and other school personnel. Such a truism is consistent with the continuity concern of unesed-apied to search for ways and means to provide for the lifelong development of teacher through in-service education. This is so the teaching process will be a dynamic force in contributing to the improvement of education in general.

For developing new professional competencies and skills in teachers in response to changes in the curriculum, and assisting teachers to solve problems of the school and community, such as drop-outs and under-achievers.

Why Schools?

1. The school is the largest and the most appropriate unit for educational change.
2. Teachers have the capability to develop their personal and professional capacities in the school and in the community.

3. Teachers need to be involved in the identification and articulation of their own training needs.
4. Individual schools have their unique needs and problems which demand unique solutions and training as well.
5. The school is a potent tool in developing its resources, both human and material.

Results:

It is a general feeling in all countries that continuing education of teachers is necessary if they are to respond adequately to the needs of the schools.

Since the in-service training requires time, efforts and funds, the crucial question is - What type of training will obtain the desired results and be based on the realities of the needs of the schools.

Solving school-oroblems through SBIT modules

1. **Improvement of Personal Skills:** Communication skills, content of learning areas, attitudes and values towards teaching and teaching processes, commitment and performance standards, knowledge of current issues and knowledge of one's mission in life as a citizen and as a professional.
2. **Upgrading of Professional Competence:** Those related to the teaching/learning process, research orientation, problem-solving, curriculum development, planning and development of educational programmes, evaluation and others.
3. **Knowledge of Teaching of Learning Areas:** Ethics education, social-studies, agriculture, value education and others.

4. **Curricular Modifications:** It includes changes due to rising demands brought about by social and technological changes.
5. **Problem-Solving:** It includes areas such as dropouts, low-achieving, and repetition rate.
6. Developing Familiarity with Innovative Projects
7. Operations of Management and in-service education programme
8. Advancement of individual teacher's experience as a professional.

Thus due to technological changes, in-service training is inevitable and cannot be ignored in educational improvement effort.

The success of SBIT module depends upon the following conditions -

1. Genuine interest and support on the part of the school leadership.
2. Trainers are component of learning reform change agents who have been well trained.
3. The office of the educational service areas must be ready to cooperate.
4. The main objective of SBIT is to create learning reform change agents for further expansion of learning reform network
5. Central agencies should prepare the necessary teacher development manuals for distribution to the schools.

Model of SBT for In-service Teacher-development

Process Methodology
Practitioner
/Responsible
Persons Meeting for Collective

P(Plan) Planning for SBT of Teachers Principal!
Academic Affair Staff

Identification of Problem/Needs
For training through questionnares/
Interview of trainees

Training
organisers/
trainers Preparation of training projects
Organising to provide knowledge and training
(Do)D Understanding of the content agreed
upon a variety of training models

Trainer/Trainees

Practical work with teaching-learning
material

(C) Check Noting observations of change
in class-room, problems or obstacles
encountered

Trainees

Periodic observations of behavior of
trainees and students in accord with
the training programme, preparing
a summary of observations

Trainers

collective sonsultation for analysis
of the observations made and
problems identified collective
recommendations for improvement
of teaching-learning activities

Trainers/Trainees

Conducting metting/organising
exhibition/exchange of lerning
Discussion to obtain recommendations
and evaluations of the training conduction.

Principal! Academic
Affair Staff
Training organisers/ Trainers
A(Action) An analysis and findings

Principal Idetificaiton of of Problems and deficiences

Academic Staff Affair

Meeting for improvement which will be beneficial to planning for subsequent training. Trainers

Conditions for success of SBIT module requires the following:

1. Genuine interest and support on the part of the school leadership.
2. Trainers are component of learning reform change agents who have been trained.
3. The office of the educational service areas must be ready to cooperate.
4. The main objective of SBIT is to create learning reform change agents for further expansion of learning reform network.
5. Central agencies should prepare the necessary teacher development manuals for distribution to the schools.

Conclusion

The office of the Educational Council should put great efforts in the preparation of the guidelines for SBIT by benefiting from extensive documentary research as well as the experiences of Teacher Development Projects of Motivational Importance. If the SBIT model is adopted on a nationwide basis and if the Ministry of Education gives approval to the Strategic Plan for Teacher Development then only the utility, the capacity, the capability and the improvement of the today's teacher as well as learner may be achieved successfully.

Content of SBIT Programme

1. Training needs of teachers, in teaching and learning.
2. How to plan, develop and implement school - based in-service education programmes (cost, length of training, mode, areas of training)
3. Methods and techniques of teaching.
4. Philosophy of teaching academic development in major fields, other professional developments including teaching and learning or ability development related to teaching performance.
5. Learning areas of the curriculum such as liberal arts, national security and national ethics.
6. Learning areas of ethics education, social studies, science and agriculture.
7. Child growth and development
8. Evaluation-techniques
9. Strategies to improve development and reduce repetition.
10. Remedial teaching
11. Guidance and counselling
12. Human relations
13. School and community development
14. Attitudes and value development
15. Class-room management
16. Formulation of objectives.
17. Time-management
18. Philosophy and approaches to adult learning.

Strategies, Techniques, Modes and Modalities

1. Nature of problems being solved.
2. Level of readiness of clientele.

3. Resources available.
4. Readiness of trainers in the type of strategy.
5. Convenience and feasibility.
6. Time and extent of training
7. Costing.
8. Availability of funds

The strategies suggested are as follows

1. **Discussion Strategies:** To include lectures and dialogues
2. **Practical Strategic:** To include observation, demonstration, field trips etc.
3. **Group Strategies:** To include workshops, seminars, small group sessions.
4. **Creative Strategies:** To include stimulation, brain-storming, role playing and micro-teaching.
5. **Systematic Strategies:** To include research to experimental method survey.
6. **Media-Assisted Strategies:** To include instructional material, radio, TV. and video-recorders.

(12)

Modernisation of Education and My Economy

In general modernisation means application of new technologies, new approaches, new scientific methods and advancement with current changes and requirements. For a common man modernisation means industrialisation and automation. As industrialisation leads to increased production resulting in better comforts and higher standards of living modernisation of education means:

Spreading education

1. To produce educated and skilled citizens
2. To train an adequate and competent intelligentsia
3. To introduce more teaching aids to make teaching learning effective
4. To adopt western educational system
5. To adopt new approaches to its aims and processes of education
6. To improve total education to relate it to national development, national needs and national aspirations

Role of Education in the Modernisation oF India

Education has led to increased production. It has led to equalization of educational opportunities and again it has led to emotional and national integration.

In India at present education has a very special and difficult role to play out because the older values and concepts are dying out and the new ones are not yet born. The old culture has lost its values and grip on the site of loyalty, honesty, sincerity, patriotism and nationalism of the youth and the new shape of the culture is far from being clear.

If education based on morals and spiritual values on one side and science and technology on the other side, then only the modernisation of education will lead to success. And if there is lack of moral and spiritual values, then it leads to terrorism and unrest inspite of economic progress. It is well said that "material riches without toleration, compassion and wisdom may well turn into dust and ashes." India should bring science and spirituality together in harmony so that it should bring growth and development of the economy as a whole and not some fractional economic growth and development. It should be the object of modernisation of education to maintain an, accurate balance between what is valuable in the legacy inherited from the past and the needs and requirements of the present. Science brings strength, scope and swiftness whereas spirituality brings stability, sustainability and sincerity. Science today is so scientific that it doesn't have its limit but useful science with its practicability is needed in the field of labour-intensive techno spirits. Modernisation, the very aim of education has to be viewed very differently. Imparting knowledge and preparing final or finished products should be replaced by awakening of curiosity, the development of proper interests, attitude and values, and building up of essential skills such as independent study and capacity to think and judge for oneself.

India is an agricultural economy. There can be no hope of modernising the agricultural economy of the country unless the farmers are ready to adopt the modern techniques of agriculture that increases yields and move out of his conservatism.

The same is true of industry also; skilled man power is needed for the relevant research and its systematic application to agriculture, industry and other sectors of economy can only come up from development of scientific and technological education. Dynamic methods of teaching and learning are required in new educational system. As the pattern of our culture and socio-economic order is refashioned, our educational system also needs to be redesigned.

Reorganisation of Eduction

As the demand for education is increasing in India with the huge plans of socio-economic development launched by successive governments based on the principles of equality and social justice. The student population in India in the higher education sector is greater than the total population of Sweden or Switzerland. Education has to be looked upon as a national investment in human resource development. Educational system needs improvement in quality as well as in quantity.

Our present educational system has created a huge army of unemployed, underemployed and unemployable graduates. And the acquisition of a degree has come to mean a passport to a clerical or other jobs unrelated to the education and training obtained at school or college. With higher degree, in hand people have to opt for low level or manual jobs thus the vocationalisation of education has to start in schools, it will help to reduce the mad rush for college education in the liberal tradition and make young people more carriar-oriented even at young age.

It is very unfortunate that despite the tremendous growth in the number of schools, colleges and universities in India, education that should conscientize the educated about their national socio-economic and political condition and help to liberate the nation from the shackles of old systems and ways of thinking is still a dream. Neither the universalization of primary education nor the vocationalisation of higher education has been achieved. It is very sad that large sums of money spent on education are not helping anyone to draw out the best in the educated.

The manual work should be equalised to the mental work as the first step towards the reorganisation of economy and education. If the dignity of labour is realised and given importance in new schemes then only the reorganisation can take place. What do we see today is that educated refused to work with their hands and remain without work. Till now in Indian education system so many new commissions and committees have made many recommendations but not implemented. No structural changes are introduced and therefore, the old systems continue even today with almost no basic change. Thus the competitive growth has been done in Indian education, in fact tremendous growth. But such growth is not only inadequate but patently dangerous. It has to be replaced by educational development based on national priorities, national ethos and an international outlook. We can achieve this goal only when there is genuine concern for the poor and the disadvantaged in the society.

13

New Trends in Education and My Economy

Education is learning of knowledge, information and skills during the course of life. The Right to Education has been described as the basic human right. Instruction refers to the intentional facilitating of learning towards identified goals. Teaching refers to the actions of a real live instructor designed to impart learning to the students. Training refers to learning with a view towards preparing learners with specific knowledge, skills or abilities that can be applied immediately upon completion. New trends in education include:

1. E-Learning Education
2. Distance Education
3. Population Education
4. Adult Education and Social Education
5. Technical and Vocational Education
6. Distance Education through Electronic Media
7. Information Technology (IT) for Educational development

All the above mentioned new trends in education are introduced in Indian educational system. But the rapid increase in India's population does not help and it results in very little gain from these trends. The Indian education system needs to be reshaped. The exam-oriented education should be replaced by job-oriented education.

A Systematic Module for Job-oriented Education

Class I to Class V: To study the interests of the children by teachers and parents with the help of School-Economy Project.

Class VI to Class VIII: Developing the interests of the children by School-Economy Project

Class IX to Class XII: Introducing and Nurturing different streams. Schools should be classified as-

1. Schools of Arts with subjects as
   a) Drawing and Painting
   b) Arts and Crafts
   c) Music
   d) Dance
   e) Theatre and Drama
   f) Sports
2. Schools of Commerce with subjects as
   a) Business Studies
   b) Accounts
3. Schools of Economics and Economy Management with subjects as-
   a) Agricultural Economics
   b) Industrial Economics
   c) Banking
   d) National Accounting
   e) Micro and Macro Economics
   f) Indian Economics and Statistics
4. Schools of Science with practical and useful subjects
   a) Biology
   b) Physics

c) Chemistry
d) Environmental Science

5. Vocational Schools: In a developing nation like India fifty percent schools should be vocational, so that learning and earning should go together. A no. of courses with training in every type of repair work should be included in it. The examples are-
    a) Stitching and Tailoring
    b) Beauty Culture
    c) TV, Computer, every type of Machine-Repairing
    d) Office Management etc. etc.

Individualisation of Education

Todays the educational system has become very complicated and complex, which is giving rise to unrest among the parents, teachers and students. The private schools have become big business shops. And the government schools their show—off business is far beyond the reality. With very poor infra-structure in majority of the government schools, the computers, big TV screens, projectors are being supplied which is a mere national wastage. A proper and systematic approach is required to use the modern means of education. Therefore, it is very essential that individualisation of education should take place. The government should allow the children to study by their own means and efforts. They should be given permission to appear in the exam, no matter where the child is studying, whether by Internet or at home by the tutors, he/she should be allowed to fill up the form with the Board of their choice and appear in exam.

To spread education single class-room schools should exist. Education should not be a tool in the hands of a priviledged class only. Study approval should be given by the government to each and every willing person. He/she should be authorised to prepare the students for filing the form and appearing the Board and exam of their choice. This whole process will stop the misuse of government money at the name of Education. The authorities of education should undergo a proper and systematic training programme for proper and systematic growth of schools and colleges.

Equalisation of Education

As the individualisation of education is important in the same way equalisation of education is also very important. Education should be treated as Education only. Either you are a convent school student, or a government school student or an Internet student and an open school student .This discrimination should be stopped. For this we need to change our thinking. If the status of knowledge is the same they all should be treated equally. In jobs also we should not make preferences for convent educated students. Language and attitudes are getting more preferences, that's why such discriminating values develop.

Self Study Approach

Education becomes more innovative when it follows the approach of Self Exploration, self understanding, self search in Libraries, inspite of low standard guides or readymade Notes which leads to cramming only with no depth of the subject.

Education should not have any concept or Criteria of Failure

If education means facilitating, imparting, gaining, receiving, sharing and enjoying the term knowledge knowledge and knowledge only then who has entered this concept of failure in it? Putting a tag of failure on children is such a psychological crime, for which god is not going to spare this mankind. Every child matters. Every child is special. Every child is perfect. God has granted his grace to each and every individual. Then who are we to put the tag of failure on them by seeing only the academic side. It means our education system is so poor that inspite of judging their correct qualities, their correct talents we are making them psychologically weak by calling them failure.

Here the Failure is our poor system which should be changed immediately. We should give the option of as many streams as their can be, so that each and every student choose it according to his/her capacities. Inspite of correcting ourselves and our system we are blindly declaring the number of failure students every year. Till now there is no counting of such students who committed suicide on account of being failed. The whole mankind should be blamed for this who is quietly seeing this drama since education is commercialised. Education is such a noble service which expands our wisdom and vision. We at the name of modernization making education a huge business industry. Whereas it should have been served as a social service only for the growth and development of an economy.

"Educaiton is a pleasure, do not make it a stress, It is a treasure of knowledge for student's uplift and not to depres."

At the end of this book I pray to God to bring back the Gurukul type schools and colleges where educaiton was under strict discipline, strict teachers and was according to social requirement and I wish if all the services shouldn't have been commercialized.

• • •